Other titles available in the Secret Fairy range

The Secret Fairy Handbook
The Secret Fairy Party Book
The Secret Fairy Boutique
The Secret Fairy in Fairyland
Nettle's Cuddly Animal Friends
The Fairy Queen's Jewel-Sign Horoscopes
Bluebell's Dazzling Beauty Tips

First published in Great Britain in 2001 by
ORCHARD BOOKS
96 Leonard Street, London EC2A 4XD
Orchard Books Australia
Unit 31/56 O'Riordan Street, Alexandria, NSW 2015
Illustrations © Penny Dann 2001
Text © Claire Freedman 2001
The right of Penny Dann to be identified as the illustrator and
Claire Freedman as the author of this book has been asserted by
them in accordance with the Copyright, Designs and Patents Act, 1988.
A CIP catalogue record for this book is available from the British Library.
10 9 8 7 6 5 4 3 2 1
ISBN 1 84121 162 1
Printed in Singapore

The Secret Fairy

Blossom's Tea Time Party

Penny Dann and Claire Freedman

ORCHARD BOOKS

The Clumsy Fairy

It was almost time for Fairyland's May Ball.
Blossom and her fairy friends were
excitedly discussing what to wear.

"I wonder who will
be crowned May Princess
this year," Blossom said.

"Well, it won't be me!"
joked Hollyhock. "I'm so
clumsy I'd probably drop
the crown and break it!"

The other fairies all had
a fit of the giggles at this. It was true –
Hollyhock was a very clumsy and messy fairy.
But she was so friendly and funny that it didn't
matter a bit and everyone loved her.

On the morning of the ball, Hollyhock was
flying in the woods. She
was looking for some
petals to make into a
necklace and some
pretty flowers caught
her eye. Hollyhock flew
down to look at them.

But she didn't notice an old tree stump and crashed straight into it!

"Clumsy me!" she cried. "Now I've got moss stains on my skirt and I've squashed the primroses!"

As Hollyhock dusted herself down she saw something glinting amongst the leaves below. She flew down and picked it up. It was a lovely sparkly brooch.

"This belongs to Rosebud, the fashion fairy," Hollyhock gasped. "It's been missing for ages. Oh, she will be pleased I've found it."

Hollyhock rushed over to see Rosebud at once. She found her busily adding the final touches to the Fairy Queen's beautiful ball gown. Rosebud was delighted to have her brooch back.

"Well done for finding it," she told Hollyhock. "Now I can wear it to the ball tonight. Is there anything I can do to thank you?" she asked.

Hollyhock hesitated.

"I wonder, could you make me look wonderful for the ball?" she asked hopefully. "However hard I try, I always end up looking a silly mess!"

"No problem!" Rosebud replied. "I'm not Fairyland's top fashion fairy for nothing. We'll get to work at once!"

What an afternoon Hollyhock had! While one fairy styled her hair, others worked on her make-up and dress. At long last she was ready for the ball.

"Oooh!" Hollyhock gasped in amazement as she stared at her reflection in the mirror, "I don't look like me any more. I look like a... princess!"

"It's a lovely dress," Rosebud said. "Pink and purple with lilac shoes and a bag to match."

"My face looks so different too," Hollyhock said with delight.

"It's the rainbow make-up," Rosebud replied. "Wait, you need one final touch!" and she sprayed Hollyhock with the most gorgeous perfume.

Hollyhock arrived at the ball wondering what her friends might say when they saw her.

"They probably won't even recognise me," she thought. And no one did!

"Hello, Blossom! Hi, Bluebell!" Hollyhock called. "Surprise – it's me!"

But the music was so loud they couldn't hear her and just wondered who she was. Feeling disappointed, Hollyhock decided to find something to eat. The food looked delicious and she was just about to take a huge bite of strawberry cake, when she had a worrying thought.

"Knowing me, I'll spill food all down my dress and spoil it," she sighed.

She put down the cake and headed for the dance floor instead. It was crowded with fairies

whirling and swirling about. Hollyhock longed to join in but she knew what would happen if she did. She'd trip over someone's feet and end up breaking a shoe. So Hollyhock sat in a corner feeling glum, watching the other fairies enjoy themselves. Suddenly she made a decision.

She rushed home, changed into her red dress and washed off some of the make-up!

"Now I look and feel like me again," she said. "And I can have some fun!"

In no time Hollyhock was back at the ball.

"At last – you're here!" called Blossom.

"We missed you!" Bluebell said. "Never mind, you're just in time to hear who has been chosen as the May Princess."

Everyone hushed as the Fairy Queen announced the winner – Hollyhock!

"Me?" gasped Hollyhock, knocking over a table as she rushed to receive her crown from the Fairy Queen. "But I'm such a hopelessly clumsy fairy."

"And a very nice one too," the Fairy Queen said as everyone clapped.

Happily, Hollyhock helped herself to some yummy strawberry cake. And when she accidentally bumped into another fairy and sent her crown flying into the jelly, even the Fairy Queen laughed!

★ Fizzy Fairy Pop Recipes ★

> I've invented these refreshing drinks for Bluebell to serve in her beauty parlour. I sip one while I'm having my hair done! These recipes serve four fairies.

Fizzy Fairy Floats

You will need:

A bottle of cherryade
Vanilla ice cream
Hundreds and thousands
or pink sugar strands
Glasses ★ Straws

1. Fill each glass three-quarters full with cherryade.

2. Add a scoop of vanilla ice cream to each glass.

3. Sprinkle lots of hundreds and thousands or sugar strands over the ice cream.

4. Top with a straw and serve at once.

Long Green Fairy Fizz

You will need:

2 kiwi fruits ★ Lime juice cordial ★ Glasses ★ Straws
Green food colouring ★ A bottle of lemonade

1. Peel and slice the kiwi fruits. Put a few slices into each glass.

2. Pour a little lime juice cordial and a drop of the food colouring into each glass.

3. Fill the glasses up with lemonade. Add a straw to each then serve and slurp!

It's delicious!

Slurp!

So refreshing!

Party Umbrella

Bluebell tops her
fairy fizz drinks with a
pretty umbrella.

1. Gently flatten a cake case a little with your palm and cut a triangle out of the circle of paper, as shown.

2. Overlap the cut edges and tape them together, putting the tape on both sides of the umbrella.

3. Push a cocktail stick through the centre of the umbrella and out the other side, into a ball of Blu-Tack™.

⋆ Strawberry Ladybirds ⋆

You will need:

Large strawberries ★ A bar of chocolate
Greaseproof paper ★ A small clean paintbrush
A large heatproof bowl ★ A small heatproof bowl

I invented these sweet little snacks myself!

I helped with the taste testing!

What are you making?

1. Carefully remove the stalks from the strawberries. Cut them in half and lay flat-side-down on a sheet of greaseproof paper.

Don't touch—
it's hot!

Yum!

2. Break the chocolate into a small bowl. Place the small bowl inside the larger bowl and ask an adult to pour boiling water in between the two, halfway up the side. Leave for five minutes then carefully remove the small bowl. Stir the chocolate with a spoon.

Hello…?

3. Dip the tip of each strawberry half into the melted chocolate to make the ladybird's head. Lay flat-side-down on the greaseproof paper to dry.

4. Use the brush to paint on a chocolate wing-case and spots. Allow the chocolate to set before moving the finished ladybirds.

5. Arrange the ladybirds and leaves on a pretty plate and share with friends!

More tea, Violet?

This gift is just for you!

Caw!

What pretty nail tattoos! I must give these to Nettle, she'll love them.

Have you seen my other books; The Secret Fairy Handbook, Party Book, Boutique or Fairyland?

Take care of yourselves! Learn how to take care of animals too in my Animal Friends book.